Prayers for Anglicans

David Adam

kevin mayhew

Published in 2008 by

KEVIN MAYHEW LTD
Buxhall, Stowmarket, Suffolk, IP14 3BW
Tel: +44 (0) 1449 737978 Fax: +44 (0) 1449 737834
E-mail: info@kevinmayhewltd.com
www.kevinmayhew.com

9 8 7 6 5 4 3 2 1 0

ISBN 978 1 84867 026 6
Catalogue No. 1501106

Cover design by Melody-Anne Lee
Edited by Katherine Laidler
Typeset by Richard Weaver

Printed and bound in Great Britain

God be in my head, and in my understanding.
God be in my eyes, and in my looking.
God be in my mouth, and in my speaking.
God be in my heart, and in my thinking.
God be at my end, and at my departing.

Sarum Book of Hours (1514)

Contents

Introduction

The wealth of prayer used within the Church over the centuries is like a great treasure house. There are countless jewels, some old and some new, some almost 4000 years old, others sparkling fresh. They are there for our use, our guidance and to encourage us to create our own.

The majority of prayers in this book have been used for many years and by thousands of Christians to express their love and devotion to the ever-present God. These prayers are not to replace our own words but to inspire us to higher devotion and to help us affirm our belief that our God is always with us. There are times of dryness when prayer refuses to come; then it is good to remain still and quiet in the presence of God, simply affirming that God is, God is with us and God loves us. In such times of dryness we can use the words of others to say what our heart feels; sometimes a single word will lead us back to an awareness of our God who never leaves us.

Daily Prayer

After traditional prayers and a short form of daily prayer, I have suggested prayers for morning, evening and night. The pattern of Daily Prayer that I have used is well tried and tested: PACTS is a method I have taught to children and still use myself.

- **Pause in the Presence.** Be still and know God is with you.
- **Adore.** Give your love to God who created you out of love and for love.

- **Confess** where you have erred and strayed from his way and turn again to God.
- **Thank** God for all that he has given you and for his wonderful creation.
- **Supplicate**. Speak to God on behalf of others and for your own needs.

In each section of PACTS I have included short arrow prayers that can quickly be learnt by heart: heart rather than just mind because they are used in worship.

Pause in the Presence

This is the most important ingredient of all prayer. Take time to know that 'The Lord is here'. Affirm that you are in the 'Name of', in the presence, power and peace of God, Father, Son and Holy Spirit. Understand that when you draw near to God, God draws near to you. It is from this awareness that we learn that in him we live and move and have our being. I have often suggested both to learners in prayer and those who have prayed for years that this is the most important part of prayer. It is deeper than words and it is an opening of yourself to your God. Remember, God will not force himself upon you: he waits for you to invite him to share with you. This is a time of relaxed awareness: a time of lovers meeting. If you only have five minutes to give to prayer, spend at least three, if not four, of them in this affirming stillness.

Adore

Adoration is a natural outcome of being with the beloved. It is when we are aware of how wonderful and loving our God is. Adoration grows out of the stillness, out of the joy of knowing that our God is our Creator, Redeemer and Strength. Adoration shows us that God is our Maker, our Keeper and our Lover. Adoration reveals to us God's purpose for the world and for us, and that purpose is love: 'God is love, and those who abide in love abide in God, and God abides in them' (1 John 4:16).

Confess

To be in the presence of such a loving God will make us aware of how often we have failed him and not lived up to his love. We may be aware of how we have ignored our God or turned away from him. We will certainly be aware that we are not worthy of his love because of our actions, our thoughts, our failure to do what is asked of us. But love bids us welcome. Sin means turning away from God, living without any reference to God. But if we turn again – repent – then we will discover that God is ready to meet us. God is ready to forgive us and welcome us home.

Thank

For many this is a doorway to God: count your blessings, think and thank. 'Enter his gates with thanksgiving, and his courts with praise. Give thanks to him, bless his name. For the Lord is good: his steadfast love endures for ever, and his faithfulness to all generations' (Psalm 100:3, 4). It is very hard to be sad and thankful at the same time. Sadness and alienation from what is around us often comes when we fail to appreciate what we have. In the same way, emptiness often gnaws at us when we have allowed our hearts to turn away from God who gives us all that we have. Thanksgiving is good for us but, more important, it is the natural response of one who knows that the Lord is good.

Supplicate

God knows our need before we ask but God also wants us to share with him our whole life and all our concerns. It is good to know that God is concerned with our lives and with the world. God loves us and the whole of creation, and often is waiting to work in us and through us. The essence of all supplication is a deep trust in God and our readiness to say, 'Your will be done'. Behind committing all to the will of God is the awareness of God's love and his transforming power. We often end our prayers in the name of Jesus Christ our Lord, for in him we know that God expresses his love for the world: in him we shall not perish but have everlasting life.

Seasonal Prayers

Seasonal prayers often give life a rhythm or a new direction which we would lack without them. Seasonal prayers are based mainly on the life of Jesus Christ, though at all times the Father and the Holy Spirit are also working in us and in the world. Today, because the Church seasons are neglected or relegated in place of secular desires, they often lack the great impact they should have on our lives. We are actually 'festival hungry' for we no longer rejoice in the saving acts of God throughout the year. If we do not celebrate the seasons, the major festivals are often left empty or without much content. The layout of the Church year is for our benefit and for our delight; it is good to enter fully into it.

The Stations of the Cross

The Stations of the Cross are found in the Anglican, Catholic and Lutheran traditions. They may be used at any time of the year but especially on Fridays in Lent and on Good Friday. They make a good personal devotion and can be used for meditation using just one or two stations a day or spending time to travel to all of the stations.

The Stations of the Cross began in Jerusalem on the Via Dolorosa, the Sorrowful Way, where pilgrims sought to stop, pray and meditate at various places where tradition said certain events happened. Some of the stations had no basis in Scripture, though the events they describe could well have happened, and were used to illustrate the fullness of the saving acts. The non-Scriptural stations are the three falls of Jesus, Jesus meeting his mother, and Veronica wiping his face. The stations were found in artwork or carvings all over Europe by the fifteenth century. Possibly the devotion arose especially for pilgrims who could not hope to travel to Jerusalem. The Stations of the Cross have provided a visual devotion for countless Christians. The number of stations has varied – some would restrict them to the biblically based stations – but usually there are now the fourteen stations.

Above all, it must be remembered that the stations are an act of pilgrimage: this is not an intellectual exercise but an act of devotion. The heart and the imagination have to be able to come into play. The stations are a journey in awareness not only of historical events but of 'the lamb that was slain before the foundation of the world' (Revelation 13:8); awareness of the presence of the Lord in our lives, in our suffering and in suffering humanity. The Way of the Cross travels through our world and is present wherever someone is betrayed by a kiss, or deserted by loved ones; wherever anyone suffers injustice or enters into darkness. Christ is found with the poor and the powerless, with the scorned and rejected. In the midst of all life the Lord is there. The Way of the Cross is a journey with our Lord. It is a journey into the love of God as revealed in his Son Jesus Christ. The crucified one knows our troubles and he is with us always.

David Adam

Unless otherwise indicated,
prayers in this book
are by David Adam.

Traditional Prayers

In the name of the Father
and of the Son
and of the Holy Spirit.
Amen.

The Lord's Prayer

Our Father, who art in heaven,
hallowed be thy name.
Thy kingdom come.
Thy will be done,
on earth as it is in heaven.
Give us this day our daily bread.
And forgive us our trespasses,
as we forgive those who trespass against us.
And lead us not into temptation,
but deliver us from evil.
For thine is the kingdom,
the power and the glory,
for ever and ever.
Amen.

The Kyrie

Lord, have mercy.
Lord, have mercy.

Christ, have mercy.
Christ, have mercy.

Lord, have mercy.
Lord, have mercy.

The Apostles' Creed

I believe in God, the Father almighty,
creator of heaven and earth,
and in Jesus Christ, his only Son our Lord,
who was conceived by the Holy Spirit,
born of the Virgin Mary,
suffered under Pontius Pilate,
was crucified, died and was buried;
he descended to the dead.
The third day he rose again;
he ascended into heaven;
he is seated at the right hand of the Father,
and will come to judge the living and the dead.

I believe in the Holy Spirit,
the holy catholic Church,
the communion of saints,
the forgiveness of sins,
the resurrection of the body,
and the life everlasting.
Amen.

Gloria

Glory to the Father and to the Son
and to the Holy Spirit:
as it was in the beginning, is now
and shall be for ever.
Amen.

The Grace

The grace of our Lord Jesus Christ,
the love of God,
and the fellowship of the Holy Spirit
be with us all always.

2 Corinthians 13:13

Morning Prayer

Pause in the Presence

In the Presence and Peace of God,
Father, Son and Holy Spirit.

Silence and affirmation

The Lord is here:
his spirit is with us.

Adoration

Glory to God in the highest,
and on earth peace to people of goodwill.
We praise you.
We bless you.
We worship you.
We glorify you.
We give thanks to you for your great glory.

From the Gloria in Excelsis

or

Bless the Lord, O my soul,
and all that is within me, bless his holy name.
Bless the Lord, O my soul,
and do not forget all his benefits –
who forgives all your iniquity,

who heals all your diseases,
who redeems your life from the Pit,
who crowns you with steadfast love and mercy.

Psalm 103:1-4

Confession

In the stillness make your confession and then say:

May Almighty God have mercy upon *me*,
forgive *me* my sins
and bring *me* to eternal life,
through Jesus Christ our Lord.
Amen.

Thanksgiving

It is good to give thanks to the Lord,
to sing praises to your name, O Most High;

to declare your steadfast love in the morning
and your faithfulness by night.

For you, Lord, have made me glad by your work;
at the works of your hands I sing for joy.

Psalm 92:1, 2, 4

Supplication

That this day may be holy, good and joyful:
we pray to you, O Lord.
That we may offer you our worship and our work:
we pray to you, O Lord.
That we may strive for the well-being of all creation:
we pray to you, O Lord.
That in the pleasures and pains of life
we may know the love of Christ and be thankful:
we pray to you, O Lord.
That we may be bound together by the Holy Spirit,
in communion with *[N and]* all your saints,
entrusting one another and all our life to Christ:
we pray to you, O Lord.
Let us commend ourselves,
and all for whom we pray,
to the mercy and protection of God.

Daily Prayer, Common Worship

Pray for the Church,
the world,
your family and loved ones,
the sick and needy
and the faithful departed.

Almighty and everlasting God,
we thank you that you have brought us safely
to the beginning of this day.
Keep us from falling into sin
or running into danger,
order us in all our doings
and guide us to do always
what is righteous in your sight;
through Jesus Christ our Lord.
Amen.

Daily Prayer, Common Worship

The Lord's Prayer (page 13)

The Grace or a Blessing (page 15 or 127)

Evening Prayer

Pause in the Presence

In the light and love of God, Father,
Son and Holy Spirit.

Silence and affirmation

The Lord is here:
his Spirit is with us.

Adoration

We praise you, O God,
we acclaim you as the Lord;
all creation worships you,
the Father everlasting.
To you all angels, all the powers of heaven,
the cherubim and seraphim, sing in endless praise:
Holy, holy, holy Lord, God of power and might,
heaven and earth are full of your glory.

From the Te Deum Laudamus

or

Praise God, from whom all blessings flow;
praise him, all creatures here below;
praise him above, ye heavenly host;
praise Father, Son and Holy Ghost.

Thomas Ken (1637–1710)

Confession

Most merciful God,
we confess to you,
before the whole company of heaven and one another,
that we have sinned in thought, word and deed
and in what we have failed to do.
Forgive us our sins,
heal us by your Spirit
and raise us to new life in Christ.

Daily Prayer, Common Worship

Thanksgiving

God our Creator, our centre, our friend,
we thank you for our good life,
for those who are dear to us,
for our dead,
and for all who have helped and influenced us.
We thank you for the measure of freedom we have,
and the extent to which we control our lives;
and most of all we thank you for the faith that is in us,
for our awareness of you and our hope in you.
Keep us, we pray you, thankful and hopeful
and useful until our lives shall end.

A New Zealand Prayer Book –
He Karakia Mihinare o Aotearoa (1989)

Supplication

Pray for all those whom you have met this day,
those you have worked with,
those you live with
and all who need your prayers.

Watch, thou dear Lord,
with those who wake, or watch, or weep tonight,
and give your angels charge over those who sleep.
Tend your sick ones, Lord Christ,
rest your weary ones,
bless your dying ones,
soothe your suffering ones,
pity your afflicted ones,
shield your joyous ones.
I ask all this for your love's sake.

St Augustine of Hippo (354–430)

Lighten our darkness, Lord, we pray;
and in your mercy defend us
from all perils and dangers of this night:
for the love of your only Son,
our Saviour Jesus Christ.
Amen.

Daily Prayer, Common Worship

The Lord's Prayer (page 13)

The Grace or a Blessing (page 15 or 127)

Night Prayer

from Compline (Common Worship)

The Lord Almighty grant us a quiet night and a perfect end.
Amen.

Save us, O Lord, while waking,
and guard us while sleeping,
that awake we may watch with Christ
and asleep may rest in peace.

Into your hands, O Lord, I commend my spirit.
Into your hands, O Lord, I commend my spirit.
For you have redeemed me, Lord God of truth.
I commend my spirit.
Glory to the Father and to the Son,
and to the Holy Spirit.
Into your hands, O Lord, I commend my spirit.

Visit this place, O Lord, we pray,
and drive far from it the snares of the enemy;
may your holy angels dwell with us
and guard us in peace,
and may your blessing be always upon us;
through Jesus Christ our Lord.
Amen.

or

Be present, O merciful God,
and protect us through the silent hours of this night,
so that we, who are wearied
by the changes and chances of this fleeting world,
may rest upon your eternal changelessness;
through Jesus Christ our Lord.
Amen.

In peace we will lie down and sleep;
for you alone, Lord, make us dwell in safety.

The Lord bless us and watch over us;
the Lord make his face shine upon us
and be gracious to us;
the Lord look kindly on us and give us peace.

Daily Prayers

Pause in the Presence

In the grace and goodness of God, Father, Son and Holy Spirit.

In your presence there is fullness of joy.

Psalm 16:11

There is none like you, O Lord;
you are great, and your name is great in might.

Jeremiah 10:6

Still me, Lord;
still my heart:
still my mind;
still my soul;
that I may be
aware of your love,
alert to your beauty,
and alive to your life.
Still me, Lord.

In the Peace, Presence, Power of God.
In the Love, Light, Leading of God.
In the Grace, Goodness and Guiding of God.

Breathe in me, Holy Spirit,
that I may think what is holy.
Move in me, Holy Spirit,
that I may do what is holy.
Attract me, Holy Spirit,
that I may love what is holy.
Strengthen me, Holy Spirit,
that I may guard what is holy.
Guard me, Holy Spirit,
that I may keep what is holy.

St Augustine of Hippo (354–430)

Speak, Lord, for your servant is listening.

1 Samuel 3:9

Surely the Lord is in this place.
The Lord is here: his Spirit is with me.
God made me, loves me and protects me.
The Lord is my light and my salvation.

Lord, make me see thy glory in every place.

Michelangelo (1475–1564)

I rest in the presence of the Creator.
I rest in the love of the Redeemer.
I rest in the power of the Spirit.
I abide in the Holy Three.
I rejoice that God is with me.

Lord, awaken my heart to your love;
open my eyes to your presence.
Creator, surround me.
Christ, abide with me.
Spirit, enfold me.
Holy God, be with me now and always.

Lord, give me stillness.
Still my mind.
Still my body.
Still my heart.
Deliver me from emptiness.
Fill me with your presence.
Let me be alive and alert
and aware of you and your love.

Adore

My Lord and my God.

John 20:28

Lord, you know that I love you.

John 21:16

Glory to God in the highest heaven, and on earth peace among those whom he favours.

Luke 2:14

My soul magnifies the Lord, and my spirit rejoices in God my Saviour.

Luke 1:46, 47

I will extol you, my God and King, and bless your name for ever and ever.

Psalm 145:1

I will praise the Lord as long as I live; I will sing praises to my God all my life long.

Psalm 145:2

Holy, holy, holy is the Lord of hosts; the whole earth is full of his glory.

Isaiah 6:3

Holy, holy, holy, Lord God the Almighty, who was and is and is to come.

Revelation 4:8

You are worthy, our Lord and God, to receive glory and honour and power, for you created all things, and by your will they existed and were created.

Revelation 4:11

Hallelujah! For the Lord our God the Almighty reigns. Let us rejoice and exult and give him the glory.

Revelation 19:6, 7

Lord, let the flame of your love
set my whole heart on fire.
May I wholly burn towards you,
wholly love you,
set aflame by you.

St Augustine of Hippo (354–430)

You, Christ, are the King of glory,
the eternal Son of the Father.
When you took our flesh to set us free
you humbly chose the Virgin's womb.
You overcame the sting of death
and opened the kingdom of heaven to all believers.
You are seated at God's right hand in glory.

From the Te Deum Laudamus

O love ever burning and never extinguished,
my God, set my heart on fire with love for you.

St Augustine of Hippo (354–430)

Set our hearts on fire with love for you, O Christ,
that in its flame we may love you
with all our heart,
with all our mind,
with all our soul,
and with all our strength,
and our neighbour as ourselves,
so that, keeping your commandments,
we may glorify you,
the giver of all good gifts.

Kontakion for Love, Eastern Orthodox

My God,
I pray that I may know you and love you,
that I may rejoice in you.
And if I may not do so fully in this life,
let me go steadily on
to the day when I come to the fullness of life.
Meanwhile, let my mind meditate
on your eternal goodness,
let my tongue speak of it,
let my heart live it,
let my mouth proclaim it,
let my soul hunger for it,
and my whole being desire it,
until I enter into your joy.

St Anselm of Canterbury (1033–1109)

O Love, O God, who created me,
in your love recreate me.
O Love, who redeemed me,
fill up in me whatever part of your love
has fallen into neglect within me.
O Love, O God, who first loved me,
grant with my whole heart,
and with my whole soul,
and with my whole strength,
I may love you.

St Gertrude (c.1256–1302)

To God the Father, who first loved us,
and made us accepted in the Beloved;
to God the Son, who loved us,
and washed us from our sins in his own blood;
to God the Holy Ghost,
who sheds the love of God abroad in our hearts,
be all love and glory,
in time and for eternity.

Thomas Ken (1637–1711)

Blessing and honour, thanksgiving and praise,
more than we can utter,
more than we can conceive,
be unto thee, O holy and glorious Trinity,
Father, Son and Holy Spirit,
by all angels, all men, all creatures,
for ever and ever.

Lancelot Andrewes (1555–1626)

What shall I give you, Lord,
in return for your kindness?
Glory to you for your love.
Glory to you for your patience.
Glory to you for forgiving us all our sins.
Glory to you for coming to save our souls.
Glory to you for your incarnation in the virgin's womb.
Glory to you for your bonds.
Glory to you for receiving the cut of the lash.
Glory to you for accepting mockery.
Glory to you for your crucifixion.
Glory to you for your burial.
Glory to you for your resurrection.
Glory to you that you were preached to all.
Glory to you in whom they believed.

St Ephrem the Syrian (c.306–373)

Eternal God,
helper of the helpless,
comforter of the comfortless,
hope of the afflicted,
bread of the hungry,
drink of the thirsty,
and Saviour of all who call upon you:
I bless and glorify your name.
I adore your goodness and delight in your love.
Take from me every tendency towards sin and vanity;
let my desires soar upwards to your love,
that I may hunger and thirst
for the bread of life and the wine of heaven,
and to know no love but yours.

Jeremy Taylor (1613–1667)

Blessed be God, the only God,
three persons in one eternity of love:
Blessed be God.
Blessed be God, the lover of humankind,
our Creator, Redeemer and Sanctifier:
Blessed be God.
Blessed be God, the fount of human love,
by whom all our common life is made fruitful:
Blessed be God.
Blessed be God, for all that he is:
Blessed be God.
Blessed be God, for all that he has done:
Blessed be God.
Blessed in the fellowship of his Church
and blessed amid the celestial host:
Blessed be God.
Blessed in the chorus of all humanity,
and blessed by the whisper of each single soul:
Blessed be God.
Blessed from everlasting, blessed now,
and blessed for ever:
Blessed be God.

Ancient Agape Liturgy

Confess

Have mercy on me, O God,
according to your steadfast love;
according to your abundant mercy blot out my transgressions;
Wash me thoroughly from my iniquity
and cleanse me from my sin.

Psalm 51:1, 2

We look for peace, but find no good;
for a time of healing, but there is terror instead.
We acknowledge our wickedness, O Lord,
the iniquity of our ancestors,
for we have sinned against you.

Jeremiah 14:19b, 20

Heal me, O Lord, and I shall be healed; save me, and I shall be saved; for you are my praise.

Jeremiah 17:14

O Lord, hear; O Lord, forgive; O Lord, listen and act and do not delay!

Daniel 9:19

Father, I have sinned against heaven and before you.

Luke 15:18

Jesus, Master, have mercy upon us!

Luke 17:13

God be merciful to me, a sinner!

Luke 18:13

Lord Jesus Christ,
Son of the living God,
have mercy on me a sinner.

The Ancient Jesus Prayer

Jesus, Lamb of God, have mercy on us.
Jesus, bearer of our sins, have mercy on us.
Jesus, redeemer of the world, grant us peace.

O Lord, forgive what I have been,
sanctify what I am,
and order what I shall be.

Holy God,
holy and strong One,
holy and immortal One,
have mercy upon us.

Most merciful God,
Father of our Lord Jesus Christ,
we confess that we have sinned
in thought, word and deed.
We have not loved you with our whole heart.
We have not loved our neighbours as ourselves.
In your mercy
forgive what we have been,
help us to amend what we are,
and direct what we shall be;
that we may do justly,
love mercy,
and walk humbly with you, our God.
Amen.

Daily Prayer, Common Worship

Forgive me my sins, O Lord;
forgive me the sins of my youth and the sins of my age,
the sins of my soul and the sins of my body,
my secret and my whispering sins,
my presumptuous and my crying sins,
the sins I have done to please myself,
and the sins I have done to please others.
Forgive me the sins which I know,
and those sins which I know not;
forgive them, O Lord,
forgive them all of thy great goodness.

Lancelot Andrewes (1555–1626)

Holy God, we confess to you,
and before the whole company of heaven;
that we have sinned in thought, word and deed
and in what we have left undone.
Forgive us, restore us
and keep us in your peace.
Amen.

Thank

My soul may praise you and not be silent.
O Lord my God, I will give thanks to you for ever.

Psalm 30:12

I give thanks to you, O Lord my God,
with my whole heart,
and I will glorify your name for ever.
For great is your steadfast love towards me;
you have delivered my soul from the depths of Sheol.

Psalm 86:12, 13

O Lord, you are my God: I will exalt you,
I will praise your name;
for you have done wonderful things.

Isaiah 25:1

I will extol you, O God my King,
and bless your name for ever and ever.
Every day I will bless you and praise your name
for ever and ever.

Psalm 145:1, 2

Amen! Blessing and glory and wisdom and thanksgiving and honour and power and might be to our God for ever and ever! Amen.

Revelation 7:12

Yours, O Lord, are the greatness, the power,
the glory, the victory, and the majesty;
for all that is in the heavens and on the earth is yours;
yours is the kingdom, O Lord . . .
And now, our God, we give thanks to you and praise your glorious name.

1 Chronicles 29:11, 13

Praise the Lord for he is good; for his steadfast love endures for ever.

Psalm 106:1

Father, I thank you for having heard me.

John 11:42

Thanks be to God, who gives us the victory through our Lord Jesus Christ.

1 Corinthians 15:57

Thanks be to you, my Lord Jesus Christ,
for all the benefits you have won for me,
for all the pains and insults you have borne for me.
O most merciful Redeemer, Friend and Brother,
may I know you more clearly,
love you more dearly,
and follow you more nearly,
day by day.

St Richard of Chichester (1197–1253)

A general thanksgiving

Almighty God, Father of all mercies,
we thine unworthy servants
do give thee most humble and hearty thanks
for all thy goodness and loving-kindness to us
and to all men.
We bless thee for our creation, preservation,
and all the blessings of this life;
but above all for thine inestimable love in the
redemption of the world by our Lord Jesus Christ,
for the means of grace, and for the hope of glory.

And, we beseech thee,
give us that due sense of all thy mercies,
that our hearts may be unfeignedly thankful,
and that we show forth thy praise,
not only with our lips, but in our lives;
by giving up ourselves to thy service,
and by walking before thee in holiness
and righteousness all our days;
through Jesus Christ our Lord,
to whom with thee and the Holy Ghost
be all honour and glory, world without end.

The Book of Common Prayer (1662)

Glorificamus Te

I offer thee
every flower that ever grew,
every bird that ever flew,
every wind that ever blew – Good God!

Every thunder rolling,
every church bell tolling,
every leaf and sod – *Laudamus Te!*
I offer thee

every wave that ever moved,
every heart that ever loved
thee, thy Father's Well-beloved – Dear Lord!
Every river dashing,

every lightning flashing
like an angel's sword – *Benedicimus Te!*
I offer thee

every cloud that ever swept
o'er the skies, and broke and wept
in rain, and with the flowerlets slept – My King!

Each communicant praying,
every angel staying
before thy throne to sing – *Adoramus Te!*

I offer thee
every flake of virgin snow,
every spring of earth below,
every human joy and woe – My love!

O Lord! And all thy glorious
self o'er death victorious,
throned in heaven above – *Glorificamus Te!*

Ancient Irish Prayer

Thanks be to you, Lord God,
for all that you have given me,
for the wonders and beauty of this world
and for life itself.
Above all, I thank you for your presence
and your love that is ever with me.

Supplicate

Lord, teach us to pray.

Luke 11:1

Not my will but yours be done.

Luke 22:42

Rise up, O Lord; O God, lift up your hand;
do not forget the oppressed.

Psalm 10:12

Lord, save us! We are perishing!

Matthew 8:25

We bring before you, O Lord,
the troubles and perils of peoples and nations,
the sighing of prisoners and captives,
the sorrows of the bereaved,
the necessities of strangers,
the helplessness of the weak,
the despondency of the weary,
the failing powers of the aged.
O Lord, be near to each;
for the sake of Jesus Christ our Lord.

St Anselm of Canterbury (1033–1109)

O Lord my God, listen to the prayer of your servant; hear my cry and grant me the requests I bring before you today.

1 Kings 8:28

Most gracious Father, we humbly beseech thee
for thy holy catholic Church.
Fill it with all truth; in all truth with all peace.
Where it is corrupt, purge it;
where it is in error, direct it;
where anything is amiss, reform it;
where it is right, strengthen and confirm it;
where it is in want, furnish it;
where it is divided and rent asunder,
make up the breaches of it,
O thou most Holy One of Israel.

Archbishop William Laud (1573–1645)

We humbly beseech thee, of thy goodness, O Lord,
to comfort and succour all them
who in this transitory life are in trouble, sorrow,
need, sickness, or any other adversity:
help us to minister to them thy strength
and consolation,
and so endow us with the grace of sympathy and
compassion that we may bring them both help
and healing: through Christ our Lord.

The Book of Common Prayer (1662)

God, grant to the living, grace;
to the departed, rest;
to the Church, the Queen, the Commonwealth,
and to all mankind, peace and concord;
and to us and all his servants, life everlasting.

Elizabethan prayer

Into your hands, O Father and Lord,
I commend my soul and body,
my parents and home,
my family, friends and neighbours,
all people of faith and love,
all who stand in special need.
Lighten our lives with your holy grace
and the knowledge of your constant presence,
O Lord in Trinity, God everlasting.

St Edmund of Abingdon (1175–1240)

Lord, we pray to you,
knowing that you watch over us.
You not only created our souls and made our bodies,
you are the Saviour, Ruler and Guide of all people.
You love us so much
that you give us reconciliation and peace.
Be kind to us, Lord;
help and heal those who are ill;
cure their diseases;
and raise up those who are depressed.
We glorify your holy Name
through Jesus Christ, your only Son.
By him may all power and glory be yours,
in the Holy Spirit, now and age after age.
Amen.

St Serapion of Thmuis (Fourth century)

Be mindful of your Church, O Lord.
Deliver it from all evil,
perfect it with your love,
sanctify it,
and gather it together from throughout the world
into the kingdom which you have prepared for it.
For yours are the power and the glory
for ever and ever.

The Didache (First or second century)

O Lord, help of the helpless,
the hope of the hopeless,
the Saviour of the storm-tossed,
the harbour of voyagers,
the physician of the sick,
we pray you.
O Lord, you know each of us and our petitions,
you know each house and its needs,
receive us all into your kingdom,
make us children of light,
and bestow your love and peace upon us.

Basil of Caesarea (c.330–379)

Grant, O Lord, that we may
live in thy fear,
die in thy favour,
rest in thy peace,
rise in thy power,
reign in thy glory;
for thy own beloved Son's sake,
Jesus Christ our Lord.

Archbishop William Laud (1573–1645)

Christ as a light illumine and guide me,
Christ as shield overshadow me.
Christ be under me, Christ be over me,
Christ beside me, on my left and my right.
This day be within and without me,
lowly and meek, yet all-powerful.
Be to the heart of each one to whom I speak,
in the mouth of each who speaks unto me,
lowly and meek, yet all-powerful.
Christ as a light, Christ as shield
Christ beside me on my left and my right.

Attributed to St Patrick (373–461)

We commend unto thee, O Lord,
our souls and our bodies,
our minds and our thoughts,
our prayers and our hopes
our health and our work,
our life and our death;
our parents and brothers and sisters,
our benefactors and friends,
our neighbours and countrymen,
and all Christian folk,
this day and always.

Lancelot Andrewes (1555–1626)

Lord Almighty, the God of our fathers,
we beseech you, hear us.

For the peace which is from above,
and for the salvation of our souls,
let us beseech the Lord.

For the peace of the whole world,
and the unity of all the holy Churches of God,
let us beseech the Lord.

For the salvation and help of all people who love Christ,
we beseech you hear us.

For our deliverance from all tribulation,
from wrath, danger, distress,
from captivity, bitter death,
and from our iniquities,
we beseech you hear us.

For the people here present,
and waiting for the rich and plenteous mercy
that is from you,
we beseech you, be merciful and generous.

Save your people, O Lord,
and bless your inheritance.
Visit your world in mercy and compassion,
we beseech you, most merciful Lord.

Hear us praying to you,
and have mercy upon us.

Liturgy of St James (Second century)

Grace at meals

Bless, O Lord, this food to our use
and our lives in your service,
and make us mindful of the needs of others.

Traditional

Come, Lord Jesus, be our guest,
and may the meal by you be blest.

Attributed to Martin Luther (1483–1546)

Blessed are you, Lord God of the Universe,
for you provide food for your people.

Be present at our table, Lord;
be here and everywhere adored.
Thy creatures bless, and grant that we
may feast in paradise with thee.

John Wesley (1703–1791)

Bless me, O Lord,
and let my food strengthen me to serve thee,
for Jesus Christ's sake.

Isaac Watts (1674–1748)

To God who gives our daily bread
a thankful song we raise,
and pray that he who sends us food
may fill our hearts with praise.

Thomas Tallis (1510–1585)

Blessed are you, Lord God of all Creation,
generously you give us the fruits of the earth
to delight and nourish us.
Bless this meal
and strengthen us in your service,
through Christ our Lord.

Traditional

Prayers for use at Communion

Christ was the Word that spake it,
he took bread and break it,
and what his word doth make it,
that I believe and take it.

Elizabeth I

Be with us, Lord, in the breaking:
in the break of day,
in the breaking of the bread,
in the breaking of our lives,
in the breaking of our hearts,
in the breaking of our hopes.
Be with us, Lord, in the breaking
for you alone can make us whole.

Be with us, Lord, in the outpouring:
in the outpouring of the wine,
in the outpouring of our hopes,
in the outpouring of our troubles.
Be with us, Lord, in the outpouring
for you alone, Lord, can make us whole.

Christ be with me, Christ within me,
Christ behind me, Christ before me,
Christ beside me, Christ to win me,
Christ to comfort and restore me.
Christ beneath me, Christ above me,
Christ in quiet, Christ in danger,
Christ in hearts of all that love me,
Christ in mouth of friend and stranger.

From St Patrick's Breastplate
translated by C. F. Alexander (1818–1895)

Grant, O Lord,
that the hands that have taken holy things
may daily bring forth the fruit of your glory.
Grant, O Lord, that the lips which have sung your praises within the sanctuary
may praise you for ever;
that the ears which have heard the music of your songs
may be closed to clamour and dispute;
that the eyes which have seen your great love
may also see your blessed hope;
that the tongues which have sung the Sanctus
may ever speak the truth.
Grant that the feet which have trod in your holy place
may always walk in the light,
and that the souls and bodies
which have tasted of your body and blood
may ever be restored in newness of life.

Liturgy of Malabar

Soul of Christ, sanctify me;
Body of Christ, save me;
Blood of Christ, flow in my veins;
Water from the side of Christ, wash me;
Passion of Christ, comfort me.
Good Jesus, hear me;
within your wounds hide me;
never let me be separated from you;
from the deadly enemy, defend me;
in the hour of my death, call me;
and ask me to come to you,
that with the saints I may sing your praise
for ever and ever.

The Anima Christi (Fourteenth century)

Prayers for the Seasons

First Sunday of Advent

Almighty God,
give us grace to cast away the works of darkness
and put on the armour of light,
now in the time of this mortal life,
in which your Son Jesus Christ came to us
in great humility;
that on the last day
when he shall come again in his glorious majesty
to judge the living and the dead,
we may rise to the life immortal;
through him who is alive and reigns with you,
in the unity of the Holy Spirit,
one God, now and for ever.

Collect for the First Sunday of Advent,
Common Worship

Day 2

Our Lord, come!

1 Corinthians 16:22

Amen. Come, Lord Jesus!

Revelation 22:20

I wait for the Lord, my soul waits,
and in his word I hope;
my soul waits for the Lord,
more than those who watch for the morning.

Psalm 130:5, 6

Day 3

Stir up your power, O Lord,
and with great might come among us;
and because we are sorely let and hindered by our sins,
let your bountiful grace and mercy speedily help
and deliver us;
through Jesus Christ our Lord.

Gelasian Sacramentary (Eighth century)

Day 4

O God of all hope and joy,
open our hearts in welcome,
that your Son Jesus Christ at his coming
may find in us a dwelling prepared for himself;
who lives and reigns with you and the Holy Spirit,
one God now and for ever.

A New Zealand Prayer Book:
He Karakia Mihinare o Aotearoa (1989)

Day 5

Come, O Lord,
open our eyes to your presence,
open our minds to your grace,
open our lips to your praises,
open our hearts to your love,
open our lives to your healing
and be known among us.

Day 6

Lord God, awaken me
to the beauty of the world
and to the wonders of creation.
Awaken me to your love
and to your coming to me this day.
As you came to the patriarchs and prophets,
you come to me:
help me to be aware of your coming.

Day 7

Hear Jesus say,
'I stand at the door and knock;
at the door of your home,
at the door of your heart,
I come to you.
Open your life to me.'

Come, Lord Jesus.

Day 8

Song

Christ is coming. Christ is coming.
Do you know? Do you know?
Are you ready for him?
Are you ready for him?
Yes, I am. Yes, I am.
Are you ready for him?
Are you ready for him?
Yes, I am. Yes, I am.

Tune: 'I hear thunder'

Day 9

Lord, awaken me to your love.
Make me aware that you come to me
today and every day.
Help me to rejoice in your coming
and in your abiding presence.

Day 10

Blessed are you, Lord my God,
for you sent messengers and prophets
to tell of your coming.
You sent John the Baptist to help us to prepare your way.
Help me to show your presence
in my daily life and in my work.

Day 11

Song

Jesus, come among us
with your glorious light.
Jesus, come among us;
help us do what's right.

Jesus, come among us;
come now and every day.
Jesus, come among us,
hear us as we pray.

Tune: Caswall, 'Glory be to Jesus'

Day 12

O Lord, you have set before us the great hope
that your kingdom shall come on earth,
and have taught us to pray for its coming:
give us grace to discern
the signs of its dawning,
and to work for the perfect day
when your will shall be done on earth
as it is in heaven;
through Jesus Christ our Lord.

The Promise of His Glory (1991)

Day 13

Come, O Christ my Light, and illumine my darkness.
Come, my Life, and revive me from death.
Come, my Physician, and heal my wounds.
Come, Flame of Divine Love,
and burn up the thorns of my sins,
kindling my heart with the flame of your love.
For you alone are my King and my Lord.

St Dimitri of Rostov (Seventeenth century)

Day 14

Come, true light.
Come, life eternal.
Come, hidden mystery.
Come, treasure without name.
Come, reality beyond all words.
Come, person beyond all understanding.
Come, rejoicing without end.
Come, light that knows no evening.
Come, unfailing expectation of the saved.
Come, raising of the fallen.
Come, resurrection of the dead.

St Symeon the New Theologian (949–1022)

Day 15

Come, all-powerful,
for unceasingly you create, refashion and change
all things by your will alone.
Come, invisible whom none may touch or handle.
Come, for you continue always unmoved,
yet at every instant you are wholly in movement;
you draw near to us who lie in hell,
yet you remain higher than the heavens.
Come, for your name fills our hearts
with longing and is ever on our lips;
yet who you are and what your nature is,
we cannot say or know.
Come, Alone to the alone.
Come, for you are yourself the desire that is within me.
Come, my breath and my life.
Come, the consolation of my humble soul.
Come, my joy, my glory, my endless delight.

St Symeon the New Theologian (949–1022)

Day 16

Come, Lord Jesus, draw near; come, Lord:
come among us.
Come as our Saviour; come, Lord:
come among us.
Come as our Friend; come, Lord:
come among us.

Come as the Light; come, Lord:
come among us.
Come and we shall be saved; come, Lord:
come among us.

Day 17

O Lord our God,
make us watchful, keep us faithful
as we wait for the coming of your Son our Lord;
that when he shall appear,
he may find us not sleeping in sin,
but active in his service and joyful in his praise;
for the glory of your holy name.

Gelasian Sacramentary (Eighth century)

Day 18

Come, Lord Jesus, Light of the World,
conquer the darkness
about me and within me.
Come, Lord Jesus.

Come Lord Jesus, Giver of Life,
conquering death,
restore me and refresh me.
Come, Lord Jesus.

Day 19

Keep us, O Lord,
while we tarry on this earth,
in a serious seeking after you
and in an affectionate walking with you,
every day of our lives;
that when you come,
we may be found not hiding our talent,
nor serving the flesh,
nor yet asleep with our lamp unfurnished,
but waiting and longing for our Lord,
our glorious God for ever.

Richard Baxter (1615–1691)

Day 20

When I close my eyes in prayer,
come, Lord Jesus.
When I cry out in the dark,
come, Lord Jesus.
When I struggle with life,
come, Lord Jesus.
When I feel lost or alone,
come, Lord Jesus.
In my celebrations and joy,
come, Lord Jesus.
In my sharing with friends,
come, Lord Jesus.

In my seeking to work for you,
come, Lord Jesus.
When I call upon your name,
come, Lord Jesus.

17 December

O Sapientia

Come with your grace and goodness;
come to my heart and change me.
Come, wisdom of God.
Come, Christ my Lord.

Come with your peace and power;
come to my life and strengthen me.
Come, wisdom of God.
Come, Christ my Lord.

Come with your light and love;
come to my darkness and enlighten me.
Come, wisdom of God.
Come, Christ my Lord.

18 December

O Adonai

Lord of the living water,
quench my thirst and refresh me.

Maranatha.
Come, Lord Jesus.

Lord of the Bread of Heaven,
fill me and strengthen me.
Maranatha.
Come, Lord Jesus.

Lord, my Friend and Saviour,
redeem me and bring me to the Promised Land.
Maranatha.
Come, Lord Jesus.

19 December

O Radix Jesse

Jesus, Word made flesh.
Maranatha.
Come, Lord, dwell among us.

Jesus, born of the house of David.
Maranatha.
Come, Lord, dwell among us.

Jesus, born of the blessed Virgin Mary.
Maranatha.
Come, Lord, dwell among us.

Jesus, from the realm of glory.
Maranatha.
Come, Lord, dwell among us.

20 December

O Clavis David

O Key of David,
you open to us your love.
Come, Lord,
be known among us.

O Key of David,
you come to set the prisoner free.
Come, Lord,
be known among us.

O Key of David,
you open to us the kingdom of heaven.
Come, Lord,
be known among us.

O Key of David,
you open to us eternal life.
Come, Lord,
be known among us.

21 December

O Oriens

The Lord is my light and my salvation;
whom then shall I fear?
The Lord is my light and my salvation.

The Lord is the stronghold of my life;
of whom shall I be afraid?
The Lord is my light and my salvation.

Psalm 27:1

Christ is the Morning Star,
who, when the night of this world is past,
brings to his saints the promise of the light of life
and opens everlasting day.

Bede (c.672–735)

O Morning Star, come;
bring light to all who are in darkness
and hope to those who face the shadow of death.

22 December

O Rex Gentium

Come to your world, O King of the Nations.
I look for you; I long for you.
I watch for you, I wait for you.

Come and rule in our hearts.
I look for you; I long for you.
I watch for you, I wait for you.

Come, be known to all people in all places.
I look for you; I long for you.
I watch for you, I wait for you.

Come, that the kingdoms of the world
may own your rule.
I look for you; I long for you.
I watch for you, I wait for you.

23 December

O Emmanuel

O Emmanuel, God with us,
open my eyes to your presence.
Maranatha.
Come, Lord Jesus.

Make my home your home.
Maranatha.
Come, Lord Jesus.

Make room in my life for you.
Maranatha.
Come, Lord Jesus.

O Emmanuel, God ever present,
reveal yourself to me.
Maranatha.
Come, Lord Jesus.

Christmas Eve

O God, who made this most hallowed night
resplendent with the glory of the true Light,

grant that we who have known the mystery
of that Light on earth,
may enter into the fullness of his joys in heaven.

Ancient Western Rite

Christmas Day

May we make room with the innkeeper
and know the joy of the shepherds,
the message of the angels,
the seeking of the wise men,
the bliss of Mary,
the presence of the Christ-child;
and may we rejoice
in the Word made flesh
dwelling among us.

26 December

O holy Child of Bethlehem,
descend to us, we pray;
cast out our sin, and enter in,
be born in us today.
We hear the Christmas angels
the great glad tidings tell:
O come to us, abide with us,
our Lord Emmanuel.

Phillips Brooks (1835–1893)

27 December

Though Christ a thousand times
in Bethlehem be born,
if he is not born in you,
you are still forlorn.

Angelus Silesius (1624–1677)

O come to my heart, Lord Jesus,
there is room in my heart for thee.

Emily Elizabeth Steele Elliott (1836–1897)

28 December

O God, I remember this day
the slaughter of the holy innocents by King Herod.
I ask your blessing upon all suffering children,
upon all innocent victims
and upon all who suffer from tyranny and violence.
I ask this in the name of him who suffered for me,
Christ my Lord.

29 December

Christ, for you there was no room at the inn;
you were taken as refugee into Egypt,
a stranger in a foreign land.

I remember before you
all who are homeless,
all refugees and wandering people.
May I remember that in sharing with them
and caring for them
I reach out to you in each of them,
Christ my Lord.

30 December

Lord Jesus, Light of the World,
I pray for peace on earth
and goodwill among all peoples.
May I learn to accept your peace,
to share your peace,
to live your peace
and to give your peace.
Lord Jesus, be known among us
and scatter the darkness from before us.

31 December

God, give us grace to accept with serenity
the things that cannot be changed,
courage to change the things that should be changed,
and the wisdom to know the difference.

Reinhold Niebuhr (1892–1971)

1 January

God bless my year with an awareness of you.

My dearest Lord,
be a bright flame before me,
a guiding star above me,
a smooth path beneath me,
and you a kindly shepherd behind me,
today and ever more.

St Columba (521–597)

2 January

Lord our God,
grant me grace to desire you with my whole heart;
that so desiring you, I may seek and find you;
and so finding you, I may love you;
and so loving you, I may hate those sins
from which you have delivered me,
through Jesus Christ our Lord.

St Anselm (1033–1109)

3 January

Eternal light, shine in our hearts;
Eternal goodness, deliver us from evil;

Eternal power, be our support;
Eternal wisdom, scatter the darkness of our ignorance;
Eternal pity, have mercy upon us;
that with all our heart and mind and strength
we may seek your face
and be brought by your infinite mercy
to your holy presence; through Jesus Christ our Lord.

Alcuin of York (735–804)

4 January

O my God, I give myself to you
in joy and in sorrow,
in sickness and in health,
in success and in failure,
in life and in death,
in time and for eternity.
Take me and keep me for your own;
through Jesus Christ my Lord.

Source unknown

5 January

Eternal God, the light of the minds that know you,
the joy of the hearts that love you,
the strength of the wills that serve you;
grant us so to know you that we may truly love you,
so to love you that we may freely serve you,
to the glory of your holy name.

St Augustine of Hippo (354–430)

Epiphany

O God, who by the leading of a star
manifested your only Son to the peoples of the earth:
mercifully grant that we,
who know you now by faith,
may at the last behold your glory face to face;
through Jesus Christ your Son our Lord,
who is alive and reigns with you,
in the unity of the Holy Spirit,
one God now and for ever.

Collect for Epiphany, Common Worship

Ash Wednesday

Almighty and everlasting God,
you hate nothing that you have made
and forgive the sins of all those who are penitent:
create and make in us new and contrite hearts
that we, worthily lamenting our sins
and acknowledging our wretchedness,
may receive from you, the God of all mercy,
perfect remission and forgiveness;
through Jesus Christ our Lord.

Collect for Ash Wednesday, Common Worship

Thursday after Ash Wednesday

Lord Jesus,
tempted to turn stones into bread,
forgive my seeking only earthly gain
and give me the vision to see
that I do not live by bread alone.
Make me aware that
I hunger for your presence
and long for your love.

Friday after Ash Wednesday

Lord Jesus,
tempted to jump from the Temple
and tempted by words of Scripture,
teach me to put my trust only in you
for you alone are the living Word
and only you can save.

Saturday after Ash Wednesday

Lord Jesus,
tempted to compromise by being offered great gain,
teach me that there is no gain
if I sacrifice or starve my soul
and that I should give my life to you;
who live and reign
with the Father and the Holy Spirit,
one God now and for ever.

First week of Lent – Dedication

Sunday

Almighty God,
whose Son fasted forty days in the wilderness,
and was tempted as we are, yet without sin:
give us grace to discipline ourselves
in obedience to your Spirit;
and as you know our weakness,
so may we know your power to save;
through Jesus Christ your Son our Lord,
who is alive and reigns with you,
in the unity of the Holy Spirit,
one God, now and for ever.

Collect for the First Sunday of Lent,
Common Worship

Monday

Grant, O Lord,
that your love may so fill our lives
that we may count nothing too small
to do for you,
nothing too much to give,
and nothing too hard to bear.

St Ignatius of Loyola (1491–1556)

Tuesday

O Lord, to turn away from you is to fall,
to turn to you is to rise,
and to stand in your presence is to live for ever.
Grant us in all our duties your help,
in all our perplexities your guidance,
in all our dangers your protection,
and in all our sorrows your peace,
through Jesus Christ our Lord.

St Augustine of Hippo (354–430)

Wednesday

Lord Jesus,
I give thee my hands to do thy work.
I give thee my feet to go thy way.
I give thee my eyes to see as thou seest.
I give thee my tongue to speak thy words.
I give thee my mind that thou mayest think in me.
I give thee my spirit that thou mayest pray in me.
Above all, I give thee my heart
that thou mayest love in me
thy Father and all mankind.

Lancelot Andrewes (1555–1626)

Thursday

Lord Jesus, our Saviour, let us now come to you.
Our hearts are cold;
Lord, warm them with your selfless love.
Our hearts are sinful;
cleanse them with your precious blood.
Our hearts are weak;
strengthen them with your joyous Spirit.
Our hearts are empty:
fill them with your divine presence.
Lord Jesus, our hearts are yours;
possess them always and only for yourself.

St Augustine of Hippo (354–430)

Friday

Lord, I am no longer my own, but yours.
Put me to what you will, rank me with whom you will.
Put me to doing, put me to enduring;
let me be employed for you or laid aside for you,
exalted for you
or brought low for you;
let me be full, let me be empty;
let me have things, let me have nothing.
I freely and wholeheartedly yield all things
to your pleasure and your disposal.
And now, glorious and blessed God,
Father, Son and Holy Spirit,
you are mine and I am yours.
So be it.

John Wesley (1703–1791)

Saturday

Father, I abandon myself to you.
Do with me as you will.
Whatever you may do with me I thank you.
I am prepared for anything.
I accept everything,
provided your will is fulfilled in me
and in all creatures.
I ask you for nothing more, my God.
I place my soul in your hands.
I give it to you, my God,
with all the love of my heart,
because I love you.
And for me it is a necessity of love,
this gift of myself,
this placing of myself
in your hands without reserve
in boundless confidence,
because you are my Father.

Charles de Foucauld (1858–1916)

Second week of Lent – Love

Sunday

Almighty God,
you show to those that are in error the light of your truth,
that they may return to the way of righteousness:
grant to all who are admitted

into the fellowship of Christ's religion,
that they may reject those things
that are contrary to their profession,
and follow all things that are agreeable to the same;
through Jesus Christ your Son our Lord,
who is alive and reigns with you,
in the unity of the Holy Spirit,
one God, now and for ever.

Collect for the Second Sunday of Lent, Common Worship

Monday

Set our hearts on fire with love for you,
O Christ our God,
that in that flame we may love you
with all our heart,
with all our mind,
with all our soul,
and with all our strength,
and our neighbours as ourselves;
so that keeping your commandments,
we may glorify you, the giver of all good gifts.

Eastern Orthodox

Tuesday

My Lord and my God, take from me
all that keeps me from you.
My Lord and my God,

grant me all that leads me to you.
My Lord and my God,
take me from myself and give me completely to you.

St Nicholas of Flue (1417–1487)

Wednesday

Look upon us, O Lord,
and let the darkness of our souls vanish
before the beams of your brightness.
Fill us with holy love,
and open to us the treasures of your wisdom.
All our desire is known to you,
and therefore perfect what you have begun,
and what your Spirit has awakened us to ask in prayer.
We seek your face; turn your face to us
and show us your glory.
Then shall our longing be satisfied,
and our peace shall be perfect.

St Augustine of Hippo (354–430)

Thursday

O Love, O God, who created me,
in your love recreate me.
O Love, who redeemed me,
fill up in me whatever part of your love
has fallen into neglect in me.

O Love, O God, who first loved me,
grant that with my whole heart,
and with my whole soul,
and with my whole strength,
I may love you.

St Gertrude (1256–c.1302)

Friday

Lord, you have taught us
that all our doings without love are nothing worth:
send your Holy Spirit
and pour into our hearts that most excellent gift of love,
the true bond of peace and all virtues,
without which whoever lives is counted dead
before you.
Grant this for your only Son Jesus Christ's sake,
who is alive and reigns with you,
in the unity of the Holy Spirit,
one God, now and for ever.

Collect for the Second Sunday after Trinity,
Common Worship

Saturday

Merciful God,
you have prepared for those who love you
such good things that pass our understanding:
pour into our hearts such love towards you

that we, loving you in all things and above all things,
may obtain your promises which exceed all that we can desire:
through Jesus Christ our Lord.

Francis Paget (1851–1911)

Third week of Lent – Guidance

Sunday

Almighty God,
whose most dear Son went not up to joy
but first he suffered pain,
and entered not into glory before he was crucified:
mercifully grant that we,
walking in the way of the cross,
may find it none other than the way of life and peace;
through Jesus Christ your Son our Lord,
who is alive and reigns with you,
in the unity of the Holy Spirit,
one God, now and for ever.

Collect for the Third Sunday of Lent,
Common Worship

Monday

O gracious and holy Father,
give us wisdom to perceive you,
intelligence to understand you,

diligence to seek you,
patience to wait for you,
eyes to behold you,
a heart to meditate upon you,
and a life to proclaim you;
through the power of the Spirit
of Jesus Christ our Lord.

St Benedict (480–550)

Tuesday

O God, the protector of all who trust in thee,
without whom nothing is strong, nothing is holy:
increase and multiply upon us thy mercy;
that thou being our ruler and guide
we may pass through things temporal,
that we finally lose not the things eternal:
Grant this, O heavenly Father,
for Jesus Christ's sake our Lord.

The Book of Common Prayer (1662)

Wednesday

Almighty and eternal God,
so draw our hearts to thee,
so guide our minds,
so fill our imagination,
so control our wills,
that we may be wholly thine,

utterly dedicated unto thee;
and then use us, we pray thee, as thou wilt,
but always to thy glory and the welfare of thy people;
through our Lord and Saviour Jesus Christ.

Archbishop William Temple (1881–1944)

Thursday

Eternal God and Father,
you create us by your power
and redeem us by your love;
guide and strengthen us by your Spirit,
that we may give ourselves in love and service
to one another and to you;
through Jesus Christ our Lord.

The Alternative Service Book (1980)

Friday

Enable us, O Lord God,
to walk in thy way with integrity and cheerfulness,
faithfully believing thy Word,
and faithfully doing thy commandments,
faithfully worshipping thee
and faithfully serving our neighbour,
in the name of thy Son our Saviour Jesus Christ.

Jeremy Taylor (1613–1667)

Saturday

O God, the protector of all who trust in you,
without whom nothing is strong, nothing is holy:
increase and multiply upon us your mercy;
that with you as our ruler and guide
we may so pass through things temporal
that we lose not our hold on things eternal;
grant this, heavenly Father,
for our Lord Jesus Christ's sake,
who is alive and reigns with you,
in the unity of the Holy Spirit,
one God, now and for ever.

Collect for the Fourth Sunday after Trinity,
Common Worship

Fourth week of Lent – The help of God

Sunday

Merciful God,
absolve your people from their offences,
that through your bountiful goodness
we may all be delivered from the chains of those sins
which by our frailty we have committed;
grant this heavenly Father,
for Jesus Christ's sake, our blessed Lord and Saviour,
who is alive and reigns with you,
in the unity of the Holy Spirit,
one God, now and for ever.

Collect for the Fourth Sunday of Lent,
Common Worship

Monday

O God, forasmuch as without you
we are not able to please you;
mercifully grant that your Holy Spirit
may in all things direct and rule our hearts;
through Jesus Christ your Son our Lord,
who is alive and reigns with you,
in the unity of the Holy Spirit,
one God, now and for ever.

Collect for the Nineteenth Sunday after Trinity,
Common Worship

Tuesday

Lord, be within me to strengthen me,
without me to preserve me,
over me to shelter me,
beneath me to support me,
before me to direct me,
behind me to bring back,
round about me to fortify.

Lancelot Andrewes (1555–1626)

Wednesday

Strengthen us, O God, to relieve the oppressed,
to hear the groans of poor prisoners,
to reform the abuses of all professions;

that many be made not poor to make a few rich:
for Christ's sake.

Oliver Cromwell (1599–1658)

Thursday

Thou hast given so much to me;
give one thing more, a grateful heart.
Not thankful when it pleases me,
as if thy blessings had spare days;
but such a heart whose very pulse
may be thy praise.

George Herbert (1593–1633)

Friday

Stay with me, Lord Jesus,
so that I shall begin to shine as you shine,
as light to others.
The light will be all from you.
It will be you who shine through me upon others.
Give light to them as well as to me;
light them with me, through me.
Help me to witness to you without preaching;
not by word but by example
and by the sympathetic influence of what I do;
by my visible resemblance to your saints
and the evident fullness of my love for you.

John Henry Newman (1801–1890)

Saturday

Give us grace, Almighty Father,
to address thee with all our hearts
as well as with our lips.
Thou art everywhere present:
from thee no secrets can be hidden.
Teach us to fix our thoughts on thee,
reverently and with love,
so that our prayers are not in vain,
but are acceptable to thee, now and always,
through Jesus Christ our Lord.

Jane Austen (1775–1817)

Fifth week of Lent – The power of God

Most merciful God,
who by the death and resurrection
of your Son Jesus Christ
delivered and saved the world:
grant that by faith in him who suffered on the cross
we may triumph in the power of his victory;
through Jesus Christ your Son our Lord,
who is alive and reigns with you,
in the unity of the Holy Spirit,
one God, now and for ever.

Collect for the Fifth Sunday of Lent,
Common Worship

Monday

O God,
the strength of all those who put their trust in you,
mercifully accept our prayers
and, because through the weakness of our mortal nature
we can do no good thing without you,
grant us the help of your grace,
that in the keeping of your commandments
we may please you both in will and deed;
through Jesus Christ your Son our Lord,
who is alive and reigns with you,
in the unity of the Holy Spirit,
one God, now and for ever.

Collect for the First Sunday after Trinity,
Common Worship

Tuesday

Almighty God,
you see that we have no power of ourselves
to help ourselves:
keep us both outwardly in our bodies
and inwardly in our souls;
that we may be defended from all adversities
which may happen to the body,
and from all evil thoughts
which may assault and hurt the soul;
through Jesus Christ our Lord.

Post-Communion Collect for the Second Sunday of Lent,
Common Worship

Wednesday

Grant, O Lord, your protection;
and in your protection, strength;
and in your strength, understanding;
and in understanding, knowledge;
and in knowledge, the knowledge of justice;
and in the knowledge of justice, the love of it;
and in that love, the love of existence;
and in the love of all existence, the love of God,
God in all goodness.

Early Welsh

Thursday

O God,
you know us to be set
in the midst of so many dangers,
that by reason of the frailty of our nature
we cannot always stand upright:
grant us such strength and protection
as may support us in all dangers
and carry us through all temptations;
through Jesus Christ your Son our Lord,
who is alive and reigns with you,
in the unity of the Holy Spirit,
one God, now and for ever.

Collect for Fourth Sunday before Lent,
Common Worship

Friday

We beseech you, Master,
to be our helper and protector.
Save the afflicted among us;
have mercy on the lowly;
raise up the fallen;
appear to the needy;
heal the ungodly;
restore the wanderers of thy people;
feed the hungry;
ransom our prisoners;
raise the sick;
comfort the faint-hearted.

St Clement of Rome (First century)

Saturday

God of might and powerfulness,
here in love and gentleness,
protect me by your goodness
from each act of sinfulness,
from each word of hurtfulness,
from each thought of evilness.
By your presence and your holiness
surround me with your gracefulness.

Palm Sunday

Lord Jesus,
as you were welcomed
when you entered into Jerusalem
with palms and shouts of praise,
we rejoice in your coming to us this day
and pray that you may enter into our lives
and the life of our community
as our Lord and King;
to you be all glory and honour,
who lives and reigns with the Father
and the Holy Spirit,
one God, now and for ever.

Holy Week

Monday

Lord,
as I remember the cleansing of the Temple,
cleanse my heart and mind
from all evil desires and thoughts.
Cleanse from your Church all that is corrupt,
that it may be a true house of prayer,
and proclaim your glory in all the world;
for your glory and for your name's sake,
Jesus my Lord and my God.

Tuesday

Lord,
as I remember today your meeting
with the disciples on the Mount of Olives,
fill my mind with the good news of the gospel
and make me aware of your power to save,
for you alone are my Lord and Saviour,
living and reigning with the Father
and the Holy Spirit,
one God, now and for ever.

Wednesday

Lord,
who rested this day at Bethany
and prepared for what lay ahead,
make me mindful of your presence
in my home and in my life.
May I not be tempted to betray you,
and may I ever be mindful
of your friendship and love;
for your glory and for your name's sake,
Jesus my Lord and my God.

Maundy Thursday

Lord Jesus
as I remember your washing of the disciples' feet,
keep me humble and ready to serve.

As I remember the Last Supper,
make me aware of your coming in the sacrament
of the Eucharist.
As I remember your betrayal,
keep my heart and life loyal to you, Christ my Lord,
who lives and reigns with the Father
and the Holy Spirit,
one God, for ever and ever.

Good Friday

O Saviour of the world,
who redeemed us by your cross and precious blood,
save us and help us, we humbly beseech you, O Lord.

The cross of Christ
defend you from all evil,
strengthen your love for him,
keep you firm in the faith,
give you comfort in your sorrows,
and rescue you from death.

Salvator Mundi

Jesus, Saviour of the world,
come to us in your mercy:
we look to you to save and help us.

By your cross and your life laid down,
you set your people free:
we look to you to save and help us.

When they were ready to perish,
you saved your disciples:
we look to you to come to our help.

In the greatness of your mercy,
loose us from our chains:
forgive the sins of all your people.

Make yourself known as our Saviour
and mighty deliverer:
save and help us that we may praise you.

Come now and dwell with us,
Lord, Jesus Christ:
hear our prayer and be with us always.

And when you come in your glory,
make us to be one with you
and to share the life of your kingdom.

Holy Saturday

Grant, Lord,
that we who are baptised into the death
of your Son our Saviour Jesus Christ
may continually put to death our evil desires
and be buried with him;

and that through the grave and gate of death
we may pass to our joyful resurrection;
through his merits,
who died and was buried and rose again for us,
your Son Jesus Christ our Lord.

Collect for Easter Eve, Common Worship

Early Easter morning

Rejoice, heavenly powers! Sing, choirs of angels!
Exult, all creation around God's throne!
Jesus Christ our King is risen!
Sound the trumpets of salvation!

Rejoice, O earth, in shining splendour,
radiant in the brightness of your King!
Christ has conquered! Glory fills you!
Darkness vanishes for ever!

On this holy night all evil is dispelled,
guilt is washed away, and peace restored.
So we are reconciled with God.
Alleluia!

From the Exsultet from the Easter Vigil

Easter Day

Today we rejoice in the salvation of the world.
Christ is risen; let us arise with him!

Christ enters new life; let us live in him!
Christ is come forth from the tomb;
let us shake off the fetters of evil!
The gates of hell are open,
the powers of evil are overcome!
In Christ a new creation is coming to birth,
Alleluia!
Let us make new.
Alleluia!

St Gregory of Nazianzus (c.330–389)

Yesterday I was crucified with Christ;
today I am glorified with him.
Yesterday I was dead with Christ;
today I am sharing in his resurrection.
Yesterday I was buried with him;
today I am waking with him from the sleep of death.

St Gregory of Nazianzus (c.330–389)

May the bright Light of Christ,
who is risen in glory,
scatter the darkness from our hearts and minds
and from this world.

Easter Week

God of life,
who for our redemption gave your only begotten Son
to death on the cross,

and by his glorious resurrection
have delivered us from the power of our enemy:
grant us to die daily unto sin,
that we may evermore live with him
in the joy of his risen life;
through Jesus Christ our Lord.

Gregorian Sacramentary

I arise today with the power of God to guide me,
the might of God to uphold me,
the wisdom of God to teach me,
the eye of God to look over me,
the ear of God to hear me,
the word of God to give me speech,
the hand of God to protect me,
the path of God to lie before me,
the shield of God to shelter me,
the host of God to defend me against the snares of the devil
and the temptations of the world,
against every one who meditates injury to me,
whether far or near.
I arise today.

Attributed to St Patrick (373–461)

Blessed be the God and Father of our Lord Jesus Christ!
By his great mercy he has given us
a new birth into a living hope
through the resurrection of Jesus Christ from the dead,
into an inheritance that is imperishable,

undefiled and unfading,
kept in heaven for us,
who are being protected by the power of God
through faith.
Blessed be God for ever.

Based on 1 Peter 1:3-5

Death has been swallowed up in victory.
Thanks be to God, who gives us the victory
through our Lord Jesus Christ.
We know that our labour is not in vain in the Lord.
Alleluia.

Based on 1 Corinthians 15:53, 57, 58

Goodness is stronger than evil;
love is stronger than hate;
light is stronger than darkness;
life is stronger than death;
victory is ours through him who loves us.

Desmond Tutu, An African Prayer Book (1995)

All shall be Amen and Alleluia.
We shall rest and we shall see,
we shall see and we shall know,
we shall know and we shall love,
we shall love and we shall praise.
Behold our end which is no end.

St Augustine of Hippo (354–430)

Almighty Father,
who in your great mercy gladdened the disciples
with the sight of the risen Lord:
give us such knowledge of his presence with us,
that we may be strengthened and sustained
by his risen life
and serve you continually in righteousness and truth;
through Jesus Christ your son our Lord,
who is alive and reigns with you,
in the unity of the Holy Spirit,
one God, now and for ever.

Collect for the Third Sunday of Easter,
Common Worship

Ascension

Blessed are you, Lord God,
for you have raised your Son
from the darkness of death
to the fullness of life eternal
and to your right hand on high.
By his death he has destroyed death;
by his rising to life again
he has restored to us eternal life;
and by his glorious ascension
he has opened for us the way to glory.
Blessed are you, Father, Son and Holy Spirit.

Pentecost

Breathe into me, Holy Spirit,
that my thoughts may all be holy.
Move in me, Holy Spirit,
that my work too may be holy.
Attract my heart, Holy Spirit,
that I may love only what is holy.
Strengthen me, Holy Spirit,
that I may defend all that is holy.
Protect me, Holy Spirit,
that I may always be holy.

St Augustine of Hippo (354–430)

Trinity Sunday

The Trinity protecting be.
The Father be over me.
The Saviour be under me.
The Spirit be about me.
The Holy Three defending me.
As evening comes, bless my home.

Holy Three, watching me.
As shadows fall, hear my call.
Sacred Three, encircle me.
So may it be. Amen to thee,
Holy Three about me.

All Saints' Day

Blessed are you, Lord our God,
for you have called us to share
with your saints in glory.
Grant that in the darkness
and evil of this world
we may be guided
by their light and example
and so serve you in joy and in love.
Blessed are you, Father, Son and Holy Spirit.

All Souls' Day

(including prayers for the departed)

O Father of all,
we pray to thee for those whom we love,
but see no longer.
Grant them thy peace;
let light perpetual shine upon them;
and in thy loving wisdom and almighty power
work in them the good purpose of they perfect will;
through Jesus Christ our Lord.

Proposed Prayer Book (1928)

Almighty God,
with whom do live the spirits of them
that depart hence in the Lord,
and with whom the souls of the faithful,

after they are delivered from the burden of the flesh,
are in joy and felicity;
we give thee hearty thanks,
for that it hath pleased thee to deliver this
our *brother/sister*
out of the miseries of this sinful world;
beseeching thee that it may please thee,
of thy gracious goodness,
shortly to accomplish the number of thine elect,
and to hasten thy kingdom;
that we, with all those that are departed in true faith
of thy holy Name,
may have our perfect consummation and bliss,
both in body and soul,
in thy eternal and everlasting glory;
through Jesus Christ our Lord.

Burial of the Dead,
The Book of Common Prayer (1549)

Bring us, O Lord, our God,
at our last awakening into the house and gate
of heaven,
to enter into that gate and dwell in that house,
where there shall be no darkness nor dazzling,
but one equal light;
no noise nor silence, but one equal music;
no fears nor hopes, but one equal possession;
no ends or beginnings, but one equal eternity;
in the habitation of thy glory and dominion
world without end.

John Donne (1572–1631)

We give them back to you, dear Lord,
who gave them to us.
Yet as you did not lose them in giving,
so we have not lost them by their return.
What you gave you take not away, O Lover of souls:
for what is yours is ours also if we are yours.

And life is eternal and love is immortal,
and death is only a horizon,
and a horizon is nothing save the limit of our sight.

Lift us up, strong Son of God, that we may see further;
cleanse our eyes that we may see more clearly;
draw us closer to yourself that we may know ourselves
to be nearer to our loved ones who are with you.

And while you prepare a place for us,
prepare us also for that happy place,
that where they are and you are, we also may be
for evermore.

William Penn (1644–1718)

Give rest, O Christ, to your servant with the saints:
where sorrow and pain are no more,
neither sighing, but life everlasting.
You only are immortal, the Creator and Maker of all:
and we are mortal, formed from the dust of the earth,
and unto earth shall we return.
For so you ordained when you created me, saying:
'Dust you are and to dust you shall return.'
All of us go down to the dust,
yet weeping at the grave we make our song:
Alleluia, alleluia, alleluia.

Give rest, O Christ, to your servant with the saints:
where sorrow and pain are no more,
neither sighing, but life everlasting.

Eastern Orthodox Kontakion for the Departed

Go forth upon your journey from this world,
O Christian soul,
in the name of him in whom you have believed,
in the name of God the Father, who created you,
in the name of Jesus Christ, who suffered for you,
in the name of the Holy Spirit, who strengthened you.
May angels and archangels and the host of heaven
come to meet you.
May all the saints of God welcome you.
May your portion this day be in gladness and peace
and your dwelling in paradise.
Go forth upon your journey, O Christian soul.

Gelasian Sacramentary

The Stations of the Cross

Begin the stations with a prayer that centres on the love of God:

In the saving power of God, Father,
Son and Holy Spirit.

Blessed are you Lord God of our salvation,
in your love for us
you gave us your Son to be our Redeemer.
As I walk the way of the cross,
may I walk with Christ our Lord
and know his great love for me.
As he gave himself for me,
help me to give my life to you,
blessed Father, Son and Holy Spirit.

After each station is named say:

I adore you, O Christ, and I bless you,
because by your holy cross
you have redeemed the world.

At the end of each station let there be a silence and then, before moving on to the next station, say:

Lord Jesus Christ,
who by your cross and passion have redeemed us,
save and help us, I humbly beseech you, O Lord.

FIRST STATION

Jesus is condemned to death

He was despised and rejected by others; a man of suffering and acquainted with infirmity . . . Surely he has borne our infirmities and carried our diseases . . . He was wounded for our transgressions, crushed for our iniquities; upon him was the punishment that made us whole, and by his bruises we are healed. All we like sheep have gone astray: we have all turned our own way, and the Lord has laid on him the iniquity of us all. He was oppressed, and he was afflicted, yet he did not open his mouth; like a lamb that is led to the slaughter, and like a sheep that before its shearers is silent, so he did not open his mouth.

Isaiah 53:3-7

The powers of this world are determined
to be rid of Jesus.
He challenges their way of life,
their power structures,
their luxury whilst others starve,
their insensitivity towards their fellows,
and for this he is condemned.

The church people are not comfortable with him.
He talks about their dedication.
He questions their lack of mission.
He wants them to love as God loves,
and for this he is condemned.

He came in love and they vent their hatred upon him.
He came to enrich their lives and they strip him
and leave him bare.
He came to give life and they condemn him to death.
He sought to set them free and they fix him to a cross
of wood.

Jesus, help me to accept you as my Lord and my God.
Increase my sensitivity to your presence in others:
help me to know that as I do it to the least of all I do
it to you.

SECOND STATION

Jesus receives the cross

'The Son of Man must undergo great suffering, and be rejected by the elders, chief priests and scribes, and be killed, and on the third day be raised.' Then he said to them all. 'If any want to become my followers, let them deny themselves and take up their cross daily and follow me. For those who want to save their life will lose it, and those who lose their life for my sake will save it. What does it profit them if they gain the whole world, but lose or forfeit themselves?'

Luke 9:22-25

Here is the cross.
Take it as if it is yours, as if you deserved it.
Take upon you the injustice, the cruelty
and the hatred of the world.

Take upon you all the pain and sorrow.
Lord, you give yourself in love –
let me not give a cross to you.

Jesus, I remember all who are forced to accept
suffering as their daily lot,
all who are betrayed by loved ones,
all deserted by their friends,
all who are very much left alone.
In you may they find hope.

THIRD STATION

Jesus falls for the first time

. . . cursed is the ground because of you; in toil you shall eat of it all the days of your life; thorns and thistles it shall bring forth for you; and you shall eat the plants of the field. By the sweat of your face you shall eat bread until you return to the ground, for out of it you were taken; you are dust, and to dust you shall return.

Genesis 3:17-19

The Son of Man is weakened;
a heart is breaking with love.
He came down to lift us up,
and now he descends to the dust.
God and dust mix together.
He humbled himself unto death,

even death on the cross.
Now he crawls in the dust – see how the dust clings to him as he arises!
He comes down to the lowest level to raise us up.

Lord Jesus, many are your humiliations:
born in a stable, taken as a refugee,
scorned and rejected, betrayed with a kiss,
denied by a friend, deserted by disciples,
brought down to the dust.
I remember before you
all who suffer humiliation and all who are brought low.

FOURTH STATION

Jesus is met by his mother

Then Simeon blessed them and said to his mother Mary, 'This child is destined for the falling and rising of many in Israel, and to be a sign that will be opposed so that the inner thoughts of many will be revealed – and a sword will pierce your own soul too.'

Luke 2:34, 35

Mary ought not to have come, but love drew her to him.
This would cost her much pain and sorrow, agony and awful memories.
Why should this happen to him, to her?
What had either done to deserve this?
There seemed to be no answer.

Pain is not a private thing; it is shared by loved ones.
If one suffers, all suffer.
Mary experiences the sword that was to pierce her heart.

Lord, I fear that if I love you,
I will be asked to walk the way of the cross.
If I give you my heart,
it will be pierced with the sorrows of the world.

FIFTH STATION

Simon of Cyrene is compelled to carry the cross

They compelled a passer-by, who was coming in from the country, to carry his cross; it was Simon of Cyrene, the father of Alexander and Rufus. Then they brought Jesus to the place called Golgotha (which means the place of the skull).

Mark 15:21, 22

Simon is an African, as Cyrene was what is now Libya.
He had no intentions of doing anything.
He was entering the city from the country.
He is forced to carry the cross.
That day he learnt something that would change him –
for we are told his sons are known by the Church.
Military rule forces its will on people.

People are still compelled to do awful things.
The cross is to be borne in our helping of the least,
in the hungry,
the refugee,
the homeless,
the outcasts.
The Lord calls us to bear one another's burdens.

Lord, as you have given your life for me,
help me to give myself to others
and to you.

SIXTH STATION

Veronica wipes the face of Jesus

Hear, O Lord, when I cry aloud,
be gracious to me and answer me!
'Come,' my heart says, 'seek his face!'
Your face, Lord, do I seek.
Do not hide your face from me.

Psalm 27:7-9

Jesus had been badly beaten.
His face is covered with sweat, dust and blood.
He is not a pretty sight.
One in the crowd is moved by his suffering.
She comes forward and stands out from the crowd.
She disregards the danger and the hostility;

she acts on impulse out of love.
It is said that the face of Jesus was captured
on the cloth she used to wipe his face.
She would keep this image in her heart.
She would remember this face, a face like any other face,
but she had looked into the eyes of God.
The face of God is scarred by thorns,
bloodied by violence.

Lord, how often I defile your image
and mar your likeness.
Forgive me and help me to reveal you to others.

SEVENTH STATION

Jesus falls a second time

My soul clings to the dust;
revive me according to your word.
My soul melts away for sorrow;
strengthen me according to your word.
Let your steadfast love come to me, O Lord,
your salvation according to your promise.
Then shall I have an answer for those who taunt me,
for I trust in your word.

Psalm 119:25, 28, 41, 42

Lord, do you never give up?
You are down again –
and I know it will not be for the last time.

How long must you suffer?
How long can your creation defile and degrade you?
Once again you bite the dust for us
and for our salvation.
Dust and divinity mingling together:
dust rising with you when you arise.

Lord, when I attach myself to you, I arise,
for with you is life and life eternal.

EIGHTH STATION

Jesus meets the women of Jerusalem

A great number of people followed him, and among them were women who were beating their breasts and wailing for him. But Jesus turned to them and said, 'Daughters of Jerusalem, do not weep for me, but weep for yourselves and for your children. For the days are surely coming when they will say, "Blessed are the barren, and the wombs that never bore, and the breasts that never nursed." Then they will begin to say to the mountains, "Fall on us"; and to the hills, "Cover us." For if they do this when the wood is green, what will happen when it is dry?'

Luke 23:27-31

Only the hardened and the toughest of people
would not be moved,
but many regimes brutalise people.

Some women are openly weeping for Jesus;
their hearts are stirred.
The mothers know a mother's heart must be breaking.
It causes tears to flow.
The sorrow of women for their children
is a great sorrow.
Jesus accepts their sympathy – but with a warning.
More than tears are needed to change the world.
If they can do this to a just man,
what will they do to others?
If this can be done to the Son of God,
then no one is safe.

Lord, I come to you in sorrow
for the suffering peoples of the world.
Give me the courage and willpower to help where I can.

NINTH STATION

Jesus falls the third time

Christ Jesus who, though he was in the form of God,
did not regard equality with God
as something to be exploited, but emptied himself,
taking the form of a slave,
being born in human likeness.
And being found in human form,
he humbled himself
and became obedient to the point of death –
even death on a cross.

Philippians 2:6-8

There you go, down again. This is becoming a habit.
You seem to be attached to the dust.
This time it looks as if this is it: are you still breathing?
Shall I count you out? I could count you out.
Are you already dead?
How long do you want to lie there: three days or more?
Death is not far away – but you rise again.

Lord Jesus, as the dust clings to you as you rise,
may I hold fast to you and to your saving power.

TENTH STATION

Jesus is stripped of his garments

My God, my God, why have you forsaken me?
Why are you so far from helping me,
from the words of my groaning? . . .
I am poured out like water,
and all my bones are out of joint;
my heart is like wax;
it is melted within my breast;
my mouth is dried up like a potsherd,
and my tongue sticks to my jaws;
you lay me in the dust of death.
For dogs are all around me;
a company of evildoers encircles me.
My hands and feet have shrivelled;
I can count all my bones.
They stare and gloat over me;
they divide my clothes among themselves,

and for my clothing they cast lots.
But you, O Lord, do not be far away!
O my help, come quickly to my aid!

Psalm 22:1, 14-19

They have taken all from you.
Now they gamble for the robe your mother gave you.
They take away your dignity and leave you exposed.
They strip you of your humanity
and will take away your life.
There is no Transfiguration, no white robes,
only bareness;
nothing to shield you from the cross or from mockery.
You are defenceless or so it seems.
Yet in love you allow all this for us.

Lord, strip from me all false pride;
strip away all self-trust;
take away all that keeps me from you.
I remember before you all who are laid bare,
all who have nothing and are counted as nothing.

ELEVENTH STATION

Jesus is nailed to the cross

So they took Jesus; and carrying the cross by himself, he went out to what is called The Place of the Skull, which in Hebrew is called Golgotha. There they crucified him, and with him two others, one on either side, with Jesus between them. Pilate also had an inscription written and put on the cross. It read, 'Jesus of Nazareth, the King of the Jews'. Many of the Jews read this inscription, because the place where Jesus was crucified was near the city; and it was written in Hebrew, in Latin and in Greek.

John 19:16b-20

Jesus who came to set them free is fixed . . .
to a cross of wood.
Listen to the sound of the nails.
Iron on iron, iron into wood, all resound.
Human flesh does not make much sound,
neither does the Son of Man.
Here is planned cruelty and indignity.
Jesus is hung like a picture – but not a pretty sight.
Arms are stretched out as if to welcome in an embrace.
This is the cost of your love, of the love of God.
The Christ is poured out for us and for our salvation.

Lord, as you open your arms to welcome me,
let me remember the cost.
By your agony and loneliness,
support me in my troubles.
By your life laid down,
lift me up and bring me to life eternal.

TWELFTH STATION

Jesus dies upon the cross

When it was noon, darkness came over the whole land until three in the afternoon. At three o'clock Jesus cried out with a loud voice, 'Eloi, Eloi, lema sabachthani?' which means, 'My God, my God, why have you forsaken me?' When some of the bystanders heard it, they said, 'Listen, he is calling for Elijah.' And someone ran, filled a sponge with sour wine, put it on a stick, and gave it to him to drink, saying, 'Wait, let us see whether Elijah will come to take him down.' Then Jesus gave a loud cry and breathed his last.

Mark 15:33-37

Can it be that God suffers for me?
Can it be that God dies for me?
The Christ has paid the extreme price of love:
he has laid down his life for us;
through him the darkness is banished.
He has served his Father faithfully even to death,
and in death he has become our Redeemer.
There is no greater love than this.

Lord Christ, my Redeemer,
as you give yourself for me and to me,
help me to give myself to you.

THIRTEENTH STATION

Jesus is taken down from the cross

When his parents saw him they were astonished; and his mother said to him, 'Child, why have you treated us like this? Look, your father and I have been searching for you in great anxiety.' He said to them, 'Why were you searching for me? Did you not know that I must be in my Father's house?'

Luke 2:48, 49

Once again Jesus returns to his mother's lap.
But there is no joy here: the body is broken
and disfigured.
A sword pierces her own heart.
How long is it since he was last in her arms?
This is a far cry from Bethlehem and Nazareth:
there was so much promise;
it seemed the whole world would follow him.
Now Jesus, her son, is dead.
He came to his own but his own received him not.
The creature has sought to kill the Creator.
What hells are let loose on the world?

Lord Christ,
I remember all who are facing death
or the death of a loved one.
I pray for all who have been killed
through violence or accidents.
Lord, in your death may *I* find hope.

FOURTEENTH STATION

Jesus is laid in the tomb

When evening had come, and since it was the day of Preparation, that is, the day before the Sabbath, Joseph of Arimathea, a respected member of the council, who was also himself waiting expectantly for the kingdom of God, went boldly to Pilate and asked for the body of Jesus. Then Pilate wondered if he were already dead; and summoning the centurion, he asked him whether he had been dead for some time. When he learned from the centurion that he was dead, he granted the body to Joseph. Then Joseph bought a linen cloth, and taking down the body, wrapped it in the linen cloth, and laid it in a tomb that had been hewn out of the rock. He then rolled a stone against the door of the tomb. Mary Magdalene and Mary the mother of Joses saw where the body was laid.

Mark 15:42-47

As the sun goes down, the Christ is buried in a borrowed grave.
After all the pain and agony he looks at rest:
the whiteness of the linen cloth helps to hide
the wounds and scars.
He lies here like a seed buried in the earth.
This is the winter of the world:
all who love him are left numbed and cold,
exhausted and empty.
At least he has passed beyond it all.

Lord Jesus, come into our darkness,
into our lives sealed against feeling,
into our many deaths.
Help me to know that you are beyond the grave
and beckon me to glory.

Lord Jesus Christ, Son of the living God,
who at this evening hour lay in the tomb
and so hallowed the grave
to be a bed of hope
for all who put their trust in you:
give us such sorrow for our sins,
which were the cause of your passion,
that when our bodies lie in the dust,
our souls may live with you for ever.

Prayer from Compline, Common Worship

Blessings and Doxologies

Go forth into the world in peace;
be of good courage;
hold fast to that which is good;
render to no man evil for evil;
strengthen the fainthearted;
support the weak;
help the afflicted;
honour all men;
love and serve the Lord,
rejoicing in the power of the Holy Spirit.
And the blessing of God Almighty,
the Father, the Son and the Holy Ghost,
be upon you,
and remain with you for ever.

Proposed Prayer Book (1928)

God the Father bless us,
Christ the Son enfold us in love,
the Holy Spirit guide us.

Lord of light, guide us;
Lord of love, enfold us;
Lord of power, protect us;
Lord of grace, go with us;
and the Holy Three bless us
now and for evermore.

The Lord bless you and keep you:
the Lord make his face to shine upon you,
and be gracious to you;
the Lord lift up his countenance upon you,
and give you peace.

Numbers 6:24-26

Grace to you and peace from God our Father and the Lord Jesus Christ.

Romans 1:7

May the God of hope fill you with all joy and peace in believing,
so that you may abound in hope by the power of the Holy Spirit.

Romans 15:13

The grace of the Lord Jesus Christ, the love of God, and the communion of the Holy Spirit be with all of you.

2 Corinthians 13:13

I pray that, according to the riches of his glory,
he may grant that you may be strengthened in your inner being with power through his Spirit.

Ephesians 3:16

I pray that Christ may dwell in your hearts through faith, as you are being rooted and grounded in love.
I pray that you may have the power to comprehend, with all the saints,
what is the breadth and length and height and depth,
and to know the love of Christ that surpasses knowledge,
so that you may be filled with all the fullness of God.

Ephesians 3:17-19

The peace of God, which surpasses all understanding,
guard your hearts and minds in Christ Jesus.

Based on Philippians 4:7

Now may our Lord Jesus Christ himself
and God our Father,
who loved us and through grace gave us eternal
comfort and good hope, comfort your hearts
and strengthen them in every good work and word.

2 Thessalonians 2:16, 17

To the King of the ages, immortal, invisible,
the only God,
be honour and glory for ever and ever. Amen.

1 Timothy 1:17

Now may the God of peace, who brought back from the dead our Lord Jesus,
the great shepherd of the sheep,
by the blood of the eternal covenant,
make you complete in everything good
so that you may do his will,
working among us that which is pleasing in his sight,
through Jesus Christ, to whom be glory for ever and ever. Amen.

Hebrews 13:20, 21

The God of grace, who has called you to his eternal glory in Christ, restore, support, strengthen and establish you. To him be glory for ever and ever. Amen.

Based on 1 Peter 5:10, 11

Grace, mercy and peace be with us from God the Father
and from Jesus Christ the Father's Son,
in truth and love.

Based on 2 John 1:3

The peace of God, which passes all understanding, keep your hearts and minds in the knowledge and love of God, and of his Son Jesus Christ our Lord:
and the blessing of God Almighty, the Father, the Son and the Holy Ghost,
be amongst you and remain with you always.

The Book of Common Prayer (1662)

May God the Father bless us;
may Christ take care of us;
the Holy Spirit enlighten us all the days of our life,
the Lord be our Defender and Keeper of body and soul,
both now and for ever, to the ages of ages.

Book of Cerne (Tenth century)

Christ the Sun of Righteousness shine upon you,
scatter the darkness from before your path,
and make you ready to meet him when he comes in glory; and the blessing of God Almighty,
the Father, the Son and the Holy Spirit,
be among you and remain with you always.

Advent Blessing, Common Worship

Christ give you grace to grow in holiness,
to deny yourself, take up your cross and follow him;
and the blessing of God Almighty, the Father, the Son and the Holy Spirit,
be among you and remain with you always.

Lent Blessing, Common Worship

The Lord bless us, and preserve us from all evil,
and bring us to everlasting life;
and may the souls of the faithful,
through the mercy of God,
rest in peace.

Sarum Primer

Christ crucified draw you to himself,
to find in him a sure ground for faith,
a firm support for hope,
and the assurance of sins forgiven;
and the blessing of God Almighty, the Father, the Son
and the Holy Spirit,
be among you and remain with you always.

Blessing for the Fifth Sunday in Lent until Wednesday in Holy Week, Common Worship

Copyright Acknowledgements